16.95

GREAT SMOKY MOUNTAINS

NATIONAL PARK

BY SANTANA HUNT

Gareth Stevens
PUBLISHING

Please visit our website, www.garethstevens.com. For a free color catalog of all our high-quality books, call toll free 1-800-542-2595 or fax 1-877-542-2596.

Library of Congress Cataloging-in-Publication Data

Hunt, Santana.
Great Smoky Mountains National Park / Santana Hunt.
    pages cm. — (Road trip: National parks)
Includes index.
ISBN 978-1-4824-1687-9 (pbk.)
ISBN 978-1-4824-1688-6 (6 pack)
ISBN 978-1-4824-1686-2 (library binding)
1. Great Smoky Mountains (N.C. and Tenn.)—Juvenile literature. 2. Great Smoky Mountains National Park (N.C. and Tenn.)—Juvenile literature. I. Title.
F443.G7H86 2015
976.8'89—dc23

2014028204

First Edition

Published in 2016 by
Gareth Stevens Publishing
111 East 14th Street, Suite 349
New York, NY 10003

Copyright © 2016 Gareth Stevens Publishing

Designer: Andrea Davison-Bartolotta
Editor: Kristen Rajczak

Photo credits: Cover, p. 1 (right) kurdistan/Shutterstock.com; cover, p. 1 (left) Dave Allen Photography/Shutterstock.com; cover, back cover, interior (background texture) Marilyn Volan/Shutterstock.com; pp. 4, 6, 8, 10, 12, 14, 16, 18, 20 (blue sign) Vitezslav Valka/Shutterstock.com; pp. 4, 6, 8, 10, 12, 14, 16, 18, 20, 21 (road) Renata Novackova/Shutterstock.com; pp. 5 (map), 21 (map) Globe Turner/Shutterstock.com; p. 5 (background) jadimages/Shutterstock.com; p. 6 Education Images/UIG/Getty Images; p. 7 Danita Delimont/Gallo Images/Getty Images; p. 9 (bottom right) Serder Uckun/iStock/Thinkstock; p. 9 (bottom left) Donald Kinsey/iStock/Thinkstock; p. 9 (top right) Rick Miller/iStock/Thinkstock; p. 9 (top left) rcimages/iStock/Thinkstock; p. 10 John Wollwerth/Shutterstock.com; p. 11 (main) DIRDPKC/iStock/Thinkstock; p. 11 (inset) Jerry Whaley/iStock/Thinkstock; p. 13 Photo 24/Stockbyte/Getty Images; p. 14 Fredlyfish4/Shutterstock.com; p. 15 (main) Betty Shelton/Shutterstock.com; p. 15 (inset) cchoc/iStock/Thinkstock; p. 16 Mark Scott/Shutterstock.com; p. 17 Kenneth Sponsler/Shutterstock.com; p. 18 Dean Pennala/iStock/Thinkstock; p. 19 Thomas Takacs/iStock/Thinkstock; p. 20 Paul Harris/The Image Bank/Getty Images; p. 21 (notebook) 89studio/Shutterstock.com.

Contents

Words in the glossary appear in **bold** type the first time they are used in the text.

Spend Time in the Mountains

The Great Smoky Mountains are found in eastern Tennessee and western North Carolina. They're part of the western Appalachian Mountains, which **stretch** from Canada to Alabama. Within the beautiful Great Smokies is the most visited US national park—Great Smoky Mountains National Park.

Great Smoky Mountains National Park is such a busy place for one interesting reason. The park is only about a day's drive away—at most—for many of those who live in the eastern third of the United States!

Pit Stop

The Cherokee people called the Great Smoky Mountains the "place of blue smoke" because of the blue-colored **haze** that surrounds the area.

All About

Great Smoky Mountains National Park

where found: eastern Tennessee and western North Carolina

year established: 1934

size: 816 square miles (2,113 sq km)

number of visitors yearly: 9 million

common wildlife: black bears, foxes, salamanders, wild turkeys

common plant life: hemlock, black walnut, azaleas, white-blossomed rhododendron

major attractions: Clingmans Dome, Laurel Falls, Appalachian National Scenic Trail

Great Smoky Mountains National Park is the largest piece of land **protected** by the US government east of the Mississippi River.

Great Smoky Mountains National Park

Nashville

MO

KY

AR

TN

MS

AL

GA

NC

SC

A Changing People

Great Smoky Mountains National Park was once part of the land occupied by the Cherokee people. White settlers arrived in the late 1700s. During the 1830s, most of the Cherokee were forced to leave this land and move west. Because so many Cherokee died, their journey is called the Trail of Tears.

By the 1900s, farms and homes had been built around the mountains. Logging was becoming big business, too. **Conservationists** worried it would cause lasting harm to the **environment**.

WELCOME
CHEROKEE INDIAN
RESERVATION

Pit Stop

The Cherokee began living in the Great Smokies more than 1,000 years ago. Some didn't leave during the Trail of Tears and have family living on the Cherokee Indian **Reservation** next to the park.

Cabins, churches, and other buildings left by settlers remain in the park for visitors to tour. You can see some of the best examples of log buildings in the eastern United States.

7

Great Biodiversity

In 1934, Great Smoky Mountains National Park was established to protect the trees and other features found in the Smokies. For a place with such **temperate** weather, the park's **biodiversity** is unusual.

One reason for this biodiversity is that weather at higher **elevations** is cooler and wetter than the land around it. So, animals and plants that like the cooler weather high in the Smokies and those that like the warm weather found below can both live in the park—just at different elevations!

Pit Stop

Scientists know of more than 17,000 species, or kinds, of plants and animals living in Great Smoky Mountains National Park and think there are a lot more they haven't found yet!

In 1976, the park was named an international biosphere reserve. This means that even more measures were put in place to care for the land. International biosphere reserves also serve as places to **research** and invent new conservation ideas.

Tree-mendous

About 95 percent of Great Smoky Mountains National Park is forest! Some parts of it have been around for thousands of years. The park is home to more than 130 tree species, more than any other United States park. That's almost as many tree species as in all of Europe, too!

Hemlocks, spruces, and other hardwood trees grow tall in the park. Until some trees lose their leaves in the fall, it can be hard to see any wildlife through them.

Pit Stop

In very wet years, it may rain as much as 7 feet (2.1 m) at the Smokies' higher elevations. That's great for the growth of forests!

By establishing a national park, the US government saved many trees from being cut down by loggers.

spring trees

11

At Home in the Park

Around 240 types of birds can be found in the park. About 120 species make their nests there, such as black-capped chickadees, Canada warblers, and winter wrens. The **endangered** red-cockaded woodpecker can be found in Great Smoky Mountains National Park, too.

In addition to birds, about 65 species of **mammals** live in the park. You can try to spot white-tailed deer, raccoons, and woodchucks, as well as a few endangered mammals, such as the Carolina northern flying squirrel and the Indiana bat.

Pit Stop

Many animals are most active at night, so viewing wildlife in Great Smoky Mountains National Park is best in the early morning and evening.

The red-cockaded woodpecker became endangered as many of the longleaf pine trees it lives in were cut down. Luckily, these trees are protected in Great Smoky Mountains National Park.

13

Salamanders and Bears, Oh My!

If you visit Great Smoky Mountains National National Park, you might see a black bear! With about 1,500 American black bears living on its land, the park is the biggest natural protected area for these mammals.

The park is known for its extraordinary numbers of another animal, too: salamanders! It's home to the most kinds of salamanders in the world. There are 31 species! Salamanders play an important role in their environment. Their presence shows an **ecosystem** is healthy, which is good news for Great Smoky Mountains National Park!

salamander

Of the 31 species of salamanders, 24 don't have lungs!

Pit Stop

If you see a black bear, don't get any closer than you already are. Slowly back away. In most cases, the bear will, too.

Chasing Waterfalls

The heights of the Great Smoky Mountains and lots of rain lead to something wonderful for visitors—waterfalls! There are several trails around the park that lead to these amazing sights.

The 80-foot (24 m) Laurel Falls gets its name from the mountain laurel, a plant that blooms near the falls in the spring.

Hen Wallow Falls is 90 feet (27 m) high, but if the winter is really cold, the water rushing down it will freeze! It creates a cool, icy sight.

Pit Stop

Abrams Falls and Grotto Falls are two other waterfalls you can visit in Great Smoky Mountains National Park.

Abrams Falls

Laurel Falls can be a busy place in the park. It's popular because it's so beautiful!

17

Clingmans Dome

Clingmans Dome shouldn't be missed on a road trip to Great Smoky Mountains National Park. It's the highest point in the park—and in the state of Tennessee!

Rising 6,643 feet (2,025 m), the top of Clingmans Dome can be challenging for visitors to reach. You can drive most of the way, but the road ends in a very steep walk to a tower built at the top. Once you reach it, though, you'll be able to see unbeatable views of the Great Smokies.

view from Clingmans Dome

Pit Stop

The Chimney Tops Trail is another steep hike in the park. It's only 2 miles (3.2 km) long—but the end is so steep, many people don't make it to the top!

On very clear days, visitors can see more than 100 miles (161 km) from the top of Clingmans Dome.

Traveling Through

Many visitors to Great Smoky Mountains National Park see the many plants, animals, and views on foot. There are about 800 miles (1,290 km) of trails to choose from! The famous Appalachian Trail even runs through the park. For those who would rather complete this part of their road trip in a car, the Blue Ridge Parkway shows off the Smokies' lovely views, too.

However you see Great Smoky Mountains National Park is up to you. You'll remember its natural beauty long after your trip is over!

Pit Stop

The Appalachian National Scenic Trail is 2,184 miles (3,515 km) long and stretches through the Appalachian Mountains. Some people have hiked the whole thing!

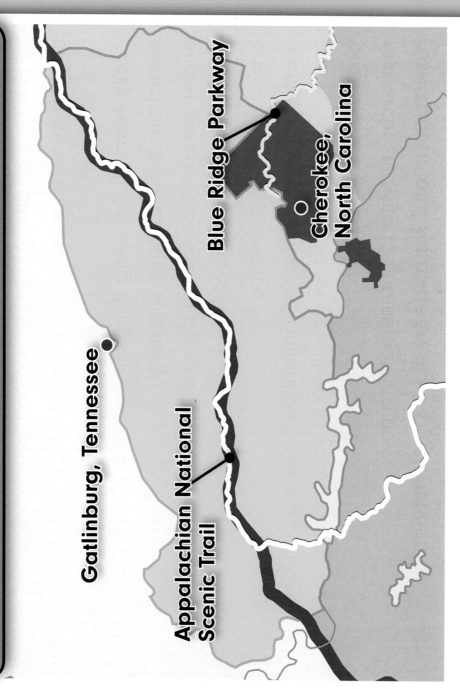

Gatlinburg, Tennessee

Blue Ridge Parkway

Cherokee, North Carolina

Appalachian National Scenic Trail

Great Smoky Mountains National Park

Cherokee Indian Reservation

Nantahala National Forest

Glossary

biodiversity: the different kinds of life in an environment shown by numbers of different kinds of plants and animals

conservationist: a person concerned with conservation, or the care of nature

ecosystem: all the living things in an area

elevation: height above sea level

endangered: in danger of dying out

environment: the natural world in which a plant or animal lives

haze: cloudy appearance

mammal: a warm-blooded animal that has a backbone and hair, breathes air, and feeds milk to its young

protect: to keep safe

research: studying to find something new

reservation: land set aside by the US government for Native Americans

stretch: to reach across

temperate: not too hot or too cold

For More Information

Books

Frisch, Nate. *Great Smoky Mountains National Park.* Mankato, MN: Creative Paperbacks, 2014.

National Geographic Society. *National Geographic Kids National Parks Guide U.S.A.: The Most Amazing Sights, Scenes, and Cool Activities from Coast to Coast.* Washington, DC: National Geographic Society, 2012.

Websites

For Kids: Great Smoky Mountains National Park
www.nps.gov/grsm/forkids/index.htm
Learn about things kids can do at Great Smoky Mountains National Park and get book recommendations, too.

Great Smoky Mountains National Park
travel.nationalgeographic.com/travel/national-parks/great-smoky-mountains-national-park/
This website has information, pictures, and even a quiz about Great Smoky Mountains National Park.

Index